YOU ARE
PRECIOUS

by
Alma Kern

Illustrated by

D1367788

ACKNOWLEDGEMENTS

Biblical references marked RSV are from the Revised Standard Version of the Bible, copyrighted 1946, 1952 © 1971, 1973. Used by permission.

Verses marked TLB are taken from THE LIVING BIBLE © 1971. Used by permission of Tyndale House Publishers, Inc., Wheaton, IL 60189. All rights reserved.

Unless otherwise stated, Scripture quotations in this publication are from the HOLY BIBLE, NEW INTERNATIONAL VERSION®. Copyright ©1973, 1978, 1984 by International Bible Society. Used by permission of Zondervan Publishing House.

Copyright ©1995 International Lutheran Women's Missionary League, 3558 S. Jefferson Avenue, St. Louis, MO 63118-3910.

Library of Congress Cataloging in Publication Data

*I thank God
for my husband —
his sound advice,
his encouragement,
and most of all,
his patient love.*

*He helps me
remember
I am precious.*

Table of Contents

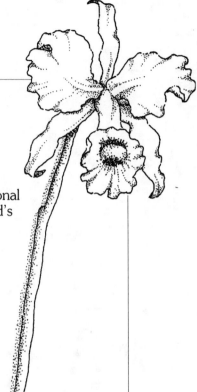

Dear Reader,

Here is a wonderful, personal message for you from God's Holy Word:

*". . . You are precious
in my eyes,
and honored,
and I love you."*

Isaiah 43:4a RSV

Know it in your head.
Stow it in your heart.
Show it in your life.

You Are Precious

God loves you just as you are.
He loves you —
not because of the good you've done —
but despite the bad things you've done
and the good you've failed to do.

You are not worthy of God's love.
Because He is holy, God insists that you be holy.
But like everybody else
you fail to meet His demand for perfection.
By nature you're hostile to Him. You can't help it.

God understands your dilemma.
He has provided a solution.

God loves you so much that He sacrificed His holy Son.
Jesus lived the perfect life required of you.
He died the death you deserved.
He suffered the God-forsakenness of hell for you.

If you believe this from the heart,
you can assure yourself:
> Jesus shed His blood for me.
> Though I am not worthy,
> I am of enormous worth.
>
> I am precious in God's eyes,
> and honored,
> and He loves me!

Your Worth

What determines
how precious
anything is?

The price
someone
is willing
to pay for it.

*". . . You were
redeemed . . .
with the
precious
blood of
Christ."*
(1 Peter 1:18-19a)

That's how
precious
you are to God!

You're an Original

At birth you received a special gift, a package deal.
Your ancestry determined your birthdate, birthplace,
ethnic group, skin color, frame size, hair texture,
intelligence, predisposition to certain diseases,
and a myriad of other qualities.

Think how many ancestors you had!
Two parents, four grandparents, eight great-grandparents,
16, 32, 64, 128, 256, 512, 1024 in ten generations!
If you could trace all your forefathers and foremothers
back 500 years, you'd find about 32,000 ancestors!
Each contributed one cell — at random — toward making you.

No wonder you are a unique, unrepeatable miracle!
There is nobody else exactly like you.
Never was. Never will be.
You can be identified by the DNA
in a drop of your blood or saliva,
a strand of hair, or any bit of body tissue.

You did not select the genes you'd inherit.
Yet you are not just a happenstance of nature.
God made you. You are His gift.
"Know that the Lord is God.
It is he who made us, and we are his." (Psalm 100:3a)

Thank the Lord for all He has given you.
Make the most of what you are and have.
You're all you've got to work with!

The Role Only You Can Fill

You are what you have been
in all your yesterdays.
All that you have read and heard,
said and done, and all that has
been said and done to you
have been registered in you.

You see the world through
the lens of your own experiences.

That's why the Lord needs you!
You're the only one like you.

Risk asking Him,
"Lord,
what can I do for others
because of my background?
because of my troubles?
because of my pains?"

There is a special role for you.
Watch for it!
Snatch it!

God Is Wonderful

Heaven is a perfect place.
All of us want to get there some day,
but none of us deserves to be there.
As we are by nature, we'd spoil heaven!

There is no do-it-yourself kit for salvation.
We cannot possibly earn eternal life.
There is no way for us to erase our sins.
But wonder of wonders!
God has done this for us!

To rescue us from our hopeless dilemma
Jesus, the perfect Son of God, humbled Himself
and became a man, a servant.
He left the glories of heaven
to take on the woes of the world.

Mankind's reaction to such amazing love?
They crucified Him!

But wonder of wonders!
His death was more than a murder.
Jesus' death was a sacrifice. He died in our place.

How does God want us to react?
"Believe in the Lord Jesus, and you will be saved."

(Acts 16:31)

Faith in Jesus as Savior and Lord
permits each of us to say:
He died for me. Now I live for Him.
I've been saved to serve and obey.

We are not qualified for heaven by what we do for God,
but by what God has done for us.

Isn't He wonderful!

Faith Works

I need to be still and know that God is God,
to remind myself how awesome He is.
The heavens are the work of His fingers.
He created the galaxies and keeps them spinning.
That's beyond my comprehension. But I believe it.

Another truth I cannot understand is this:
God loves me. He has chosen me to be His own.
Jesus died to make that possible. I believe it.

Faith saves! Nothing more!
Nothing less! Nothing else!

Does this mean I can just sit on my pew
and bask in God's marvelous love?
Is this why the Almighty has called me? No!
I'm God's workmanship created to do good works.

Jesus teaches me there is a time for pious acts,
and also a time to do nitty-gritty things.

I need to do whatever I can to feed the hungry,
clothe the naked, shelter the homeless,
look after the sick, and bring hope to
the imprisoned, the lonely, the discouraged.

I do this not to earn God's favor,
but because I am a channel of His love.

It's one way I can say, "Thank You."

"For it is by grace
you have been saved,
through faith —
and this is not
from yourselves,
it is the gift of God —
not by works,
so that no one can boast.

For we are God's workmanship,
created in Christ Jesus
to do good works,
which God prepared
in advance for us to do."
(Ephesians 2:8 –10)

You Are God's Gift

All you are and have are gifts from God.
Thank Him for what He has given you.
Recognize your gifts; develop them.

You are God's gift to your neighbors.
Use your gifts to share God's love with them.
Your neighbors are His gifts to you. Appreciate them.

Jesus is God's greatest gift to you.
Trust Him and eternal life is yours.
Follow Him and your life is worthwhile.

You're a Very Important Person

Do you know who you are?
If you believe Jesus is Lord,
you are God's child,
a Christ in miniature!

Jesus is with you.
In fact, He is in you.

Faith in Him will enable you
to do whatever He wants you to do.

God's love has come to you
person to person.
Pass it on — person to person.

You Are Christ's Ambassador

You represent Jesus!
The apostle Paul wrote *"We are . . . Christ's
ambassadors, as though God were making
his appeal through us."* (2 Corinthians 5:20a)

You are on special assignment.
God is trying to reach others through you.

The Lord wants you to be a channel of His love,
a witness to His saving power.

God is depending upon you.
His reputation is tied up with your conduct.

What a terrific honor!
What an awesome responsibility!

You may be the only contact some people
have ever had with Jesus.
What they believe about Him
is influenced by what you do and say.

May others see Jesus in you!

"You . . . are
a letter from Christ . . .
written not with ink
but with the Spirit
of the living God,
not on tablets of stone
but on tablets of human hearts."
(2 Corinthians 3:3)

You Can Fly

The poster shows a beautiful butterfly.
Below is a cocoon with a little black head poking out.
The caption reads, "You can fly, but the cocoon has to go."

What's holding you back?
Think of something you ought to do,
something you've wanted to do for a long time
but haven't had enough will power or courage.

Be specific. Perhaps it is:
forgiving someone who has hurt you,
giving up a bad habit or starting a good habit,
finishing some project,
coming to a decision, losing a few pounds,
improving an attitude (maybe complaining less,
being more patient),
taking a trip, or writing a certain letter.

Sometimes we procrastinate because we need help.
If necessary ask for help from someone you respect.
Procrastination is non-productive.
You get tired just thinking about what needs to be done.
Getting things done gives a sense of accomplishment.

Set one goal at a time. Have realistic deadlines.
Decide what must be done first.
What can you do about it this week? today? this hour?

Ask God for guidance and strength.
Use the strength and leading that He offers.

Remember, progress takes faith — and effort, effort!

You can do it if you want to.
You're a butterfly in the making!

God Came Down

God once entered this world in human form.
Incredible as it seems, He arrived as we all do.

Why did Jesus leave His heavenly home?
It was not to learn firsthand
how it feels to be human.
He did not come to study the world's problems,
but to provide the solution.
Jesus came down to where we are,
so that we might rise to where He is.

He experienced our trials and temptations.
He always did what was pleasing to His Father.
Yet He died as a criminal in the company of robbers.
But the grave could not contain Him.
He triumphed over death and the devil.
All this He did to pay the penalty of our sin.

God commands: *"Love the Lord your God*
with all your heart and with all your soul
and with all your mind. . . .
Love your neighbor as yourself." (Matthew 22:37,39)

No matter how hard we try to do that, we often fail.
Much of the time we fail to try.

God is just, but God is also love.
He forgives us for Jesus' sake.

True faith responds to such love with love.

"Praise be to the God and Father
of our Lord Jesus Christ,
the Father of compassion
and the God of all comfort,
who comforts us
in all our troubles,
so that we can comfort
those in any trouble
with the comfort
we ourselves have received from God.
For just as the sufferings of Christ
flow over into our lives,
so also through Christ
our comfort overflows."
                    (2 Corinthians 1:3–5)

The Healing Place

A church is similar to a hospital.
The difference is that everybody in the church
is a patient suffering with the same disease.

Symptoms vary, but the diagnosis is the same: sin.
Thanks to the Great Physician, we can escape
the eternal consequence of the malignancy.
But we do have to cope with the temporal results.

There is no complete cure.
The church can only help hold the disease in check.
Occasionally we have relapses. Symptoms flare up.
At such times church members annoy, disappoint,
disillusion, and even disgust one another.

The church must depend on its ambulatory patients
to serve as doctors, nurses, technicians, helpers.
We're all the Lord has to staff His healing place.
His directions: *"Serve one another in love."* (Galatians 5:13)
We need to comfort, encourage and challenge each other
in our common fight against the disease.

Group therapy helps control the symptoms.
We share God's prescriptions and witness to the results.
Together we exercise faith and build up our muscles.

The Lord expects us to do more than lie around
feeding ourselves and "licking our wounds."
He orders us to go outside our safe haven
to look for and bring in other spiritually sick people.
Some of them are not even aware of their sin problem.
Others recognize their symptoms but
do not know the Great Physician.

To be part of His rescue squad is not just our duty.
It is our privilege.

Invite Him In

Jesus comes to where you live —
whether it's on Wit's End Way
or the street called Success.

The Lord does not force Himself —
or His blessings — upon you.
He waits to be wanted.

"Here I am!" Jesus announces.
"I stand at the door and knock.
If anyone hears my voice and
opens the door, I will come in and
eat with him, and he with me."
                    (Revelation 3:20)

Jesus wants to become part of your life,
not to demand something from you,
but to give something to you —
the gift of Himself,
the gift of eternal friendship with Him.

Open the door of your heart.
Invite Him to come in.

Trouble Taker

Everybody has troubles
of one kind or another
at one time or another.

Some are of our own making.
We did what we shouldn't, or
failed to do what we should.

Sometimes other people cause our problem.
Many troubles are just a normal
part of our human lot.

God has not promised to keep us from trouble.
But Jesus does give the command:
"Do not let your hearts be troubled." (John 14:1)
Do not let troubles depress your spirit.
Don't let them get you down.

To innoculate ourselves against
this type of "heart trouble,"
we need to prepare ourselves.

Day after day we need to remind ourselves
of certain wonderful truths
that strengthen our hearts and minds:
> No matter what happens, God is for me.
> God is in control. He will turn evil into good.
> Jesus loves me. He is always with me.
> I can trust Him, He died for me!
> His sacrifice removed my greatest trouble —
> the eternal consequences of my sin.
> Surely He will give me the courage to cope with
> and the strength to stand up to
> whatever today or tomorrow brings.

"The troubles of my heart have multiplied;
free me from my anguish.
Look upon my affliction and my distress
and take away all my sins."
                                    (Psalm 25:17,18)

"Though you have made me see
troubles, many and bitter,
you will restore my life again;
from the depths of the earth
you will again bring me up."
                                    (Psalm 71:20)

"For he will deliver the needy
who cry out,
the afflicted who have no one to help.
He will take pity on the weak ..."
                                    (Psalm 72:12,13a)

God's Incredible Love

You don't deserve to go to heaven.
No one does!
All of us are spiritual rejects.
We could never do enough good
to make up for the bad we've done.

What we cannot do God did for us.
Jesus left His heavenly home —
not to survey our problem but to solve it.

He lived a perfect human life.
But Jesus' perfection was not tolerated.
He was rejected, persecuted, tortured.
God's Son suffered a death He did not deserve,
so we could have a life we don't deserve.

Jesus unlocked heaven's gates for us.
If we believe in the Lord Jesus,
we will be saved.
Salvation is by believing, not achieving.

What incredible love Jesus showed us!
It calls for our total commitment!

Take Time with God

Dear Lord,
I've got to make this short. I'm in a hurry.
There's more to do today than I can handle.
I need Your help. Here's what I'd like You to do.

O Lord, I'm sorry. Forgive my dither. Calm me down.
I must not come to You just to get what I want,
but to become what You want me to be.

Help me realize prayer is not an interruption,
but an investment. It links me to You —
the inexhaustible power that spins the universe.

Forgive me for praying as if I'm in charge,
"Listen, for Your supervisor is speaking."

Enable me to surrender myself and say,
"Speak, for your servant is listening." (1 Samuel 3:9b)

As I go about my busy-schedule-day,
may I remember I'm Your child. I must reflect You.
Fill me with Your Spirit, love, wisdom and strength.

Keep me mindful of the certainty
that nothing will happen to me today
that You and I together can't handle.

Prayer Moments

Often we say we have no time.
But each of us has all the time there is —
24 hours every day.
How one spends the moments makes the difference.

While doing chores that need little thought,
talk to God about the needs of others.

Making a bed takes little conscious thinking.
While doing it, pray for someone who is sick.

When you dust, pray for a person
who doesn't yet know Jesus as Savior.

As you clean up after a meal,
pray for the hungry or the lonely.

Doing laundry is less boring
if you are thanking God for your loved ones.

Having a conversation with God
while doing something else
doesn't mean prayer is of secondary importance.
It does turn spare moments into prayer moments.

Lawbreaker

"Speed Limit 55"
That's not realistic!
I try to be law-abiding,
but if I drive at 55,
I'm in everybody's way.
So I go with the flow.

O Lord, You set rules
to govern conduct
on the highway of life.
Forgive me for often
disregarding them —
adjusting my behavior
to comply with my
fellow travelers.

Light for the Darkness

Finally I saw a light
at the end of the dark tunnel.
But it was the headlight of a train,
and it was coming toward me!

Have you ever gone through such a dark period?
You just got up from one hard blow
only to be struck down by another.

One whole book of the Bible deals with this.
Job suffered tragedy after tragedy.
He complained, *"God has wronged me . . .
he has shrouded my paths in darkness."* (Job 19:6,8)
Things got so bad Job wished he'd never been born.
Yet in the midst of his troubles
Job stubbornly clung to this conviction:
*"I know that my Redeemer lives,
and that in the end he will stand upon the earth.
And after my skin has been destroyed,
yet in my flesh I will see God."* (Job 19:25,26)

God confronted Job and reminded him
that the Almighty is also all-wise.

When we are floored by the problems of life,
and cry out, "Why does God allow evil to happen?"
the best answer we can come up with is:
"God only knows."

The God who delivered us from the
eternal penalty of sin
will in all things work for the
good of those who love Him.

Our Redeemer lives!
Because He lives, we, too, shall live!
Here and now —
and hereafter.

Strength for the Day

The Lord my God
is always with me.
He is a great and
awesome God!

*"I can do everything
through him who
gives me strength."*
(Philippians 4:13)

I can take it.
I can make it.
Yes, I can.
God will help me.
Yes, He will!

Still, Small Voice

God speaks to me in words
written long ago and far away.
God's voice does not originate
only in the distant times.
Today He made His message
very clear — not in words
thundered out of the clouds.

It was spoken here and now
through the voice of a friend.
She didn't say, "I'm bringing
a message direct from God!"
In words quite unspectacular,
she said, "I'm bringing over
a hot meal."

Those simple, down-to-earth words
rang with the sound of God's voice.
He reminded me,
    "Don't be discouraged.
    You'll soon be well.
    I'm watching, providing.
    Be of good cheer!"

"For God does speak —
now one way, now another —
though man may not perceive it."
                   (Job 33:14)

Good Out of Bad

Opportunity knocks.
Sometimes it knocks hard.

Hard knocks disturb me.
Often they dishearten me.

Lord, help me
discern which
hard knocks of my life
are really opportunities.

When God Says No

Sometimes God says "No" to our prayer.
That doesn't mean He didn't hear us
or didn't reply. "No" is a valid answer.

God's "No" frustrates and disappoints us.
It might make us angry.
At times it breaks our hearts.

Even the psalmists had such reactions.
They asked God to do what they knew was good.
He failed to do it. They couldn't understand.

At times they accused God of being far away,
of not listening, sleeping on the job,
forgetting their misery. (Psalm 44:23f)

They were shockingly honest with God.
Yet no matter how mistreated or neglected they felt,
they didn't stop talking to the Lord.

We, too, can tell our heavenly Father
exactly how we feel. He knows anyway, but
it may help us to verbalize our thoughts.

The psalmist complained, *"Why have you forgotten me?"*
                                        (Psalm 42:9)
His situation didn't change; his attitude did.
*"Why are you downcast, O my soul? ... Put your hope
in God."* (Psalm 42:11)

The psalmists praised the Lord,
recalling the great and good things He had done.
Exalting Him lifted their spirit.

It will strengthen us to remind ourselves:
*"Praise the Lord, O my soul,
and forget not all his benefits."* (Psalm 103:2)

Let God Be God

"If it be Thy will."
That can roll off our tongue with no effort.
But these words are very difficult to pray
when we are begging the Lord to heal a loved one,
restore a broken relationship, help us find a job
or pay our bills.

We may try to wheedle the Lord into doing our will.
We're afraid to let God be God
lest He alter our plans, our lives.
He may ask us to do what we don't like,
give up what we enjoy having or doing.

Jesus teaches us to ask with great boldness.
We can tell God our needs and desires,
even register our complaints.
But we need to surrender our will
and rely on God's goodness and wisdom
to give whatever is best for our eternal good.

Our heavenly Father wants only good things for us.
He knows us better than we do
and loves us more than we love ourselves.

Good News!

The media feed us generously on news.
What they present as news is usually sad or bad.

We Christians know God's good news!
That's why we gather regularly —
not to concentrate on how bad we are,
but to celebrate how good God is!

Our worship service ought not be a pity party
but an outpouring of joyful thanksgiving.

Jesus died. That is sad.
Our sins helped crucify Him. That's bad.
But He isn't dead. He's alive! That's glad news!
He died in our place. That's the good news!
He's coming again! For us! That's great news!

How enthusiastic we ought to be
when we praise the Lord!
The word "enthusiasm" means God in us,
to be possessed by Him.
We are His precious possession,
honored and loved by Him. We belong to Jesus!
He is in us and with us —
whether we feel His presence or not.

Praising the Lord cannot be limited
to the hour of worship service once a week.
It has to bubble over into a life of service all week.
We'll share the good news about Jesus in word and action!

Shape Up!

Your body is a temple of the Holy Spirit.
Maintain it as well as you can to glorify Him.

The body is your "earthsuit."
It's the only one you'll get,
so take good care of it.
You can't live here without it.

We may not be too happy about the shape we're in.
We might even be disgusted and discouraged.
Often we know the rules for good health,
but tend to take the path of least resistance.

If we know what we should be doing
and fail to do it, it is a sin.
Jesus died for our sins.
He loves us through thick and thin —
even our thick and thin.

When we confess our failures, God forgives.
If we ask His help in improving ourselves,
He gives the confidence and strength we need.

Then we must exert effort! effort! effort!
Our loving heavenly Father is very wise.
Usually He does not do for us
what we can do for ourselves.

*"Strengthen
your
feeble
arms
and
weak
knees."*
    (Hebrews 12:12)

Growing His Way

What grows in the garden without help? Weeds!
Flowers need nurture and care.
Weeds thrive on neglect.

So it is in our lives.
Those of us who belong to Jesus
desire to become more and more like Him.
Yet with the apostle Paul we confess,
"I have the desire to do what is good,
but I cannot carry it out.
For what I do is not the good I want to do;
no, the evil I do not want to do —
this I keep on doing." (Romans 7:18b,19)

Satan tempts us to believe:
    "There's nothing wrong with indulging
    your human nature once in a while.
    It's normal for you to be selfish;
    if you don't look out for you, who will?
    Let your neighbor take care of himself."

Such thoughts grow like weeds in a garden.

Only the Spirit of God can transform our thinking.
But it is a struggle for us to let Him do this.
It takes day-by-day repentance and surrender.
Such surrender is not defeat.
It is the gateway to victory.

Be Encouraged

When you talk to yourself,
say an encouraging word.

You may be a disappointment
to yourself — and to God.
But the Lord sees potential in you.
He can recycle you.

When self-doubts trouble you,
remind yourself, aloud if possible:
I believe God loves me. He is for me.
I believe Jesus died for me.
I believe His Spirit can change me.
I can become what He wants me to be.

Knowing that God is on your side,
and always at your side,
will give you confidence.

Faith grants you the certain hope of eternal life.
But faith is not only a pass to heaven.
It's also a vital force for living this life.

See Your Possibilities

When you look in a mirror, smile.
You're not what you ought to be.
But there is hope!
You can be better than you now are.

There may be some things
you don't like about yourself.
There certainly are things
God doesn't like about you.
But He loves you anyway.

He wants you to love yourself,
because He wants you
to love your neighbor as yourself.
Self-love is the standard by which
you love others.

The more you show love to others,
the greater will be your self-respect.

The Lord sees possibilities in you.
See them in yourself.
It takes determination and effort to change.
But you have a tremendous advantage.
You're hooked up to the power Source!

"God ... gives power and strength
to his people. Praise be to God!"
(Psalm 68:35b)

A Point to Ponder

Why is it that
everything I eat
turns into me?

Can it be that
all I read
and everything
I watch on TV
also become
part of me?

No Has-Been

It's no fun watching your own face grow old.
We live in a culture that admires youth.
Most of us don't want to be younger.
We just want to keep from being old.

Some people won't admit their age.
They don't want others to think they're has-beens.

God decided the date you'd be born.
You don't have to apologize for your age.
If you have many candles on your cake, praise the Lord!
Life is a gift. Be thankful for every year!

Remember God put you where you are at this time —
at this stage of your life — for a purpose.
Bring a little of God's love into someone's life —
a phone call, a kind word or deed, a smile.
Loving other people helps ward off old age.
It improves your health and your sense of self-worth.

God loves you — not only when you're young and strong —
not only when you can work hard for Him.
We're apt to overemphasize what we do for God
and neglect the value of who we are to God.

You're never a has-been.
From starting gate to finish line
you are precious to your heavenly Father.

My Changeless Lord

I live in a changing body
in a changing world in changing times.

One thing doesn't change:
Jesus loves me. He is in me.
He is always with me.

I am confident of this,
that He who began a good work in me
will carry it on to completion. (Philippians 1:6)

The Lord works in me and through me.
Since He completes what He begins,
my possibilities are always
greater than my abilities.

"I know
that my Redeemer lives,
and that in the end
he will stand upon the earth.

And after my skin
has been destroyed,
yet in my flesh I will see God;
I myself will see him
with my own eyes —
I, and not another.
How my heart yearns within me!"
                    (Job 19:25-27)

A New Creation

God made and maintains heaven and earth
and sea and everything in them.
But He is never too busy to care for you.

None of your problems is too big for Him to handle.
None is too small for Him to bother with.

You didn't do anything to earn God's favor.
You are not good enough to deserve His love.
You don't have to be.
You are precious to Him because you are you,
and because He is God, and God is love.

You may have a negative attitude toward yourself.
Tragic circumstances may have convinced you life is unfair.
Perhaps a person you loved has hurt you deeply.
Maybe people you trusted disappointed you,
those who were supposed to love you neglected you.

The past cannot be changed, but you can be changed.

Ask the Lord to heal your inner hurts,
to enable you to receive His gracious love.
Believe Jesus is your best Friend.
Invite Him into your life.
Believe that united with Him you can be a new creation
with a new and positive attitude.

Cherish these words God speaks to you:
    " . . . *You are precious in my eyes,*
    and honored, and I love you . . ." (Isaiah 43:4a RSV)
Know them in your head.
Stow them in your heart.
Show them in your life.

God's Gift of Power

The Lord offers a variety of gifts,
but one gift is certain:
*"You shall receive power when the Holy Spirit
has come upon you; . . . "* (Acts 1:8a RSV)

Yet the Spirit, who filled the universe with light,
gives us only as much power as we desire,
only the power we are willing to use.

We see the principle in electric current.
Enough power is available in our homes
to heat the oven, the dryer and at the same time
operate dozens of lights and appliances.
But if only the clock is running,
very little current flows.

Sometimes we don't receive much power
from the Spirit of God
because we don't use much power.
We just coast along content as we are.
We are often just marking time,
going around in circles like clocks.

When we risk being God's kind of people,
trying to be more like Jesus,
doing things He wants us to do,
things which go against our nature,
we realize how much we need God's help.

It's always available to us.
We need only receive it and use it.

Got a Problem?

When you face a perplexing problem,
take time out to talk it over
with your heavenly Father.

Drop your troubles into God's lap.
Take your mind off your problems
and think about God.

For a few minutes meditate
on God's peace rather than the
specific details of your troubles.

This will refresh and renew you.
*"And the peace of God, which transcends
all understanding, will guard your hearts
and your minds in Christ Jesus."* (Philippians 4:7)

God will not solve all your problems.
He will not dissolve all your troubles.
But a sense of His presence
and confidence in His power and love
will keep you from falling apart.

You can survive whatever life brings,
stronger for having had a tough experience.
You'll be better equipped to tell others
what God has done for you.

Help!

A good prayer when you
>   are lonely, scared, miserable,
>   don't know which way to turn,
>   have no strength to go on, or
>   are at the end of your rope:
>   HELP!

For our prayer to be effective,
we need no formal theological language,
or long, flowery phrases.

We do need to believe:
>   God is.
>   God is here.
>   God is good.
>   He is listening.
>   He will answer
>   at the best time
>   in the best way
>   His love and wisdom
>   can devise.

God Expects Great Things of You

Take a good look at a bunch of grapes.
How in the world did all the juice and flavor
get into those grapes from that scrawny stem?

The vine draws nutrients from the earth.
Unless it is attached to the vine,
the feeble stem can do nothing.

Jesus says, *"I am the vine; you are the branches.*
If a man remains in me and I in him,
he will bear much fruit;
apart from me you can do nothing.
I chose you . . . to go . . . and bear fruit —
fruit that will last." (John 15:5,16b)

What fruit are we expected to produce?
The fruit that the Spirit works in us —
  "love, joy, peace, patience,
  kindness, goodness, faithfulness,
  gentleness and self-control." (Galatians 5:22)

If these elements are not evident in our life,
there is something wrong with our God-connection.
We need to remain closely attached to Jesus
to be all He expects us to be
and do all He expects us to do.

"... *I keep working toward that day when I will finally be all that Christ saved me for and wants me to be.*"
(Philippians 3:12b TLB)

Let God Use You

Sometimes God depends upon us.
If we let Him, He uses us to do His work.
His Spirit will empower us to do remarkable things.

When the angel came to the Virgin Mary,
he told her the Holy Spirit
would enable her to conceive the Son of God.

What a shocker that must have been!
Mary was troubled by what the angel said,
but she was willing to have the Lord use her.

The Holy Spirit did an amazing thing through Mary.
Because she believed and said, "Yes,"
the Savior of the world was born of Mary!

This miracle was a once-in-forever happening.
But God can still use ordinary people like us
to do extraordinary things —
if we believe and are willing to be used.

God's Tool

Lord Jesus,
help me look at myself
in a new way and see that
I have something to offer.

I am Your gift
to those whose lives I touch.
I can help make Your love felt.

You are in me and I in You.
When I help my neighbor,
You work through me.

I serve as a tool in Your hand.
Without me You will not.
Without You I cannot.

Together Forever

I love and obey Jesus —
not in order to be saved.
I love and obey Him
because I am saved.

Jesus gave His life for me.
I live my life for Him.
He is my Savior and also my Lord.
This assurance lightens my load.

This is my joy and confident hope:
Jesus lives! He lives with me.
He lives in me and loves through me.
Our togetherness is for eternity.

A Security System

Sometimes terrible things happen —
also to God's people.
That's to be expected.
We live in enemy-held territory.
Jesus called Satan "the prince of this world."
Evil people follow his devilish ways;
their crimes affect us all.

How should we then live?
Cowering in our corner?
Scared to death that harm might strike?

It is normal for us to be afraid at times.
Fear keeps us out of certain troubles.
It may cause us to be more cautious,
to use the common sense the Lord gave us.

Too much fear can cripple us.
It puts such a strangle hold on us
that we cannot do what ought to be done
or enjoy what life has to offer.

The best remedy for fear is faith.
The more of one, the less of the other.
Faith is a fear extinguisher.

As God's children we can be confident that
no evil will happen to us without
our loving Father's permission.
If evil does befall us, He will turn it into good.

We live in a dangerous world.
We should do everything we can
to protect ourselves, and
trust God to do what is beyond our control.

*"When
I am afraid,
I will
trust in you.
In God,
whose word I praise,
in God I trust;
I will not be afraid.
What can
mortal man do to me?"*
(Psalm 56:3,4)

*"O my Strength,
I sing praise to you;
you, O God,
are my fortress,
my loving God."*
(Psalm 59:17)

It's Great to Be Humble

How can we be humble when we know we're precious?
Actually, the more we realize how precious we are to God,
the more humble we can become.
We don't have to prove our worth. We know it.

To be humble does not mean we have low self-esteem.
It is not humility that makes one say,
"I can't do this," or "I can't do anything right."
That's poor self-image — maybe even laziness.

Self-respect is a precious possession.
It recognizes one's abilities as gifts from God.
Humility is willingness to use those gifts
for the glory of God and the good of others.

Humility is not thinking less of oneself,
but thinking of oneself less.

My Friend

What a blessing you have been!
Holding my hand
when I needed support.
Listening
when I had something to share.
Cheering me on
when my spirits drooped.
Pushing me
when I was in a rut.
Giving advice
when I really needed it.
Doing me a favor
when I had a problem.
Hugging me
when I longed to be loved.

You are God's gift to me.
I thank Him for you.

Say It and Show It

Actions speak louder than words.
That's true if what you do
contradicts what you're saying.

When you say, "I love you,"
your deeds must back it up.
But don't rely on action alone.

God gave us the wonderful ability to speak.
Words can express our thoughts precisely.

Each of us is made with a longing to love
and to be loved. We thrive on love.
Husband and wife should tell each other frequently,
"I love you."
Once in a while say, "I love you" to your
child, parent, pastor, friend.

Those words will be easier to say
if you practice them regularly.

They will be cherished if your
actions prove them.

There Is Hope

Do you feel boxed in by a hopeless situation?
Do you see no solution to your problem,
and no possibility that things will improve?

Hopelessness will get you nowhere.
When you give up hope, you fail to try.
You feel defeated and are less apt to pray.
Yet God is your hope! Reach out to Him for help.

Ask Him to strengthen your faith.
Faith in His love and power restores hope.
God-confidence gives you self-confidence.

Hope is the oxygen of the soul.
It is not the conviction that
everything will turn out the way you wish.
Hope is confident expectation that
if you trust in God and hold on,
you will get through the darkest times.

God is in control. He loves you very much.
He sent His beloved son to rescue you
from the eternal consequences of your sin.
Surely He can handle your present problem.

Perhaps He won't solve it the way you desire.
He will do what is best. Be certain of that.

*"The eyes of the Lord are on those
who fear him, on those whose hope
is in his unfailing love."* (Psalm 33:18)

70

*"Those who hope
in the Lord
will renew
their strength.
They will soar
on wings like eagles;
they will run and
not grow weary,
they will walk
and not be faint."*
(Isaiah 40:31)

Don't Worry About Tomorrow

We need to think about the future.
That's where we'll spend the rest of our life.

We need to prepare for what may lie ahead.
But we cannot be fully ready for the future,
because we cannot be certain of what will happen.

We must not borrow trouble from the future,
torturing ourselves with thoughts such as:
What if this or that happens?
What shall we eat? What shall we wear?

Living today well requires all our strength.
We must not spoil it worrying about what might be.

*"Therefore do not worry about tomorrow,
for tomorrow will worry about itself.
Each day has enough trouble of its own."* (Matthew 6:34)

Worry means we do not think God can
look after the practical details of life.

We must expect some setbacks.
Skies won't be sunny every day.
There will be clouds, rain, thunder.

But of this we can be sure:
though we may live under the shadow of clouds,
our heavenly Father is above them.

He is the same yesterday, today and tomorrow.
His love is all we can count on. It's enough!

A Safety Zone

*"I will
take refuge
in the shadow
of your wings
until the
disaster
has passed."* (Psalm 57:1b)

O Lord,
I believe
Your promise
not to leave me
or forsake me.

*"I do believe;
help me overcome
my unbelief!"* (Mark 9:24b)

" . . . make
the teaching
about God our
Savior
attractive."
   (Titus 2:10b)

"For we are
to God
the aroma of
Christ among
those who are
being saved . . ."
   (2 Corinthians 2:15a)

Be Friendly in Church

Many of us think our own church is friendly.
Groups of people stand around in conversation
before and after the service.
They make arrangements for meetings,
check up on mutual friends, swap all sorts of information.

While active members are busy talking among themselves,
the lonely, the hurting, the stranger
may come and go unnoticed.
They may leave with the empty feeling
of being unimportant and unwelcome.

Some churches have an official greeting committee.
This helps. But it is not enough.
Each member should feel responsible to greet
at least one unfamiliar person each week.

Most people want to be friendly, but they're shy.
Very few find it easy to approach a stranger.
Yet it takes very little courage to smile.
With a little practice a smile leads to a friendly word.

Too often our problem is not timidity but lack of concern.
We get so wrapped up in ourselves we don't care about others.
We don't realize how hard it is to get people
to come to church — and to keep them coming.

The church is not merely a social club — for members only.
We are to support one another but also
to reach out to attract others to our fellowship.
A smile or friendly greeting on our part
may encourage someone to draw nearer to Jesus.

Friendliness in church is more than a courtesy.
It is our responsibility!

Care to Share

"If I speak in the tongues
of men and of angels, but
have not love, I am a noisy
gong or a clanging cymbal.
And if I have . . . all knowledge . . .
but have not love, I am nothing."
(1 Corinthians 13: 1,2 RSV)

O Lord,
help me remember
my neighbors
don't really care
how much I know.

They need to know
how much
I really care.

May I care
enough
to share Your love
with them.

Be an Encourager

Have you ever been discouraged?
In spite of hard work, you doubted you could
finish what you felt must be done.
You lacked time, skill or energy.

Then God sent you an encourager,
a person who gave you a boost, a helping hand,
or perhaps just an encouraging word —
someone who loved you, believed in you,
and said so.

Ultimately the Lord is our source of help,
but often He uses people to help people.

Life is tough. It's easy to lose heart.
An encourager puts courage in us.
His caring and sharing helps
lift our sagging shoulders and spirits.

Again and again God's Word says:
"Let us encourage one another." (Hebrews 10:25)
"Encourage one another daily." (Hebrews 3:13a)
"Encourage one another and build each other up."
                              (1 Thessalonians 5:11a)

Encouragement is a double blessing.
Both giver and receiver are blessed.

Share the Blessing

There are some things I cannot do.
I couldn't sing in an opera —
no matter how much I'd want to
or how hard I tried.

Other things I could do only if I wanted to.
I could play a guitar, but I'd need instruction
and then practice, practice, practice.

I can do whatever God tells me to do.
Jesus tells me to be His witness.
He wouldn't tell me to do the impossible.

He didn't call me to be
a secret service saint!

Because He chose me to be His own,
I have peace and joy in my heart.
I know if I'd die tonight,
I would be with Jesus forever!
He wants me to share this blessing with others.

Some of my friends and neighbors
need to know Jesus is the way to heaven.

I could tell them what He means to me —
if I really wanted to.

I just need more courage, some instruction,
and then practice, practice, practice.

Keep My Lamp Burning

"I love you, O Lord, my strength. (v.1)

The Lord is my rock,
*   my fortress and*
*   my deliverer;*
my God is my rock, in whom I take refuge. (v.2a)

He reached down from on high
and took hold of me;
he drew me out of deep waters. (v.16)

You, O Lord, keep my lamp burning;
my God turns my darkness into light. (v.28)

With your help I can advance against a troop;
with my God I can scale a wall. (v.29)

As for God, his way is perfect;
the word of the Lord is flawless.
He is a shield for all who take refuge in him.
For who is God besides the Lord?
And who is the Rock except our God?
It is God who arms me with strength
and makes my way perfect. (vv.30-32)

The Lord lives! Praise be to my Rock!
Exalted be God my Savior!" (v. 46)

From Psalm 18

On Assignment

We live in a wicked world.
So did Cain and Abel. Sin is not new;
it has just multiplied with the population.

Communication has so improved
that we learn more gory details
about more evil in more places.

Moral decay is emphasized,
dramatized and glamorized.
Sin is reported with relish not revulsion
and listened to with fascination not disgust.

The bad news can scare us into panic
or, worse, make us numb with apathy.
Sometimes we're inclined to close our ears,
look the other way, rationalize, excuse.

The world needs God desperately.
That's why Jesus sends us out
with this assignment:
be the salt of the earth, the light of the world.

Salt preserves. Even a small amount added to
food gives zest and greatly improves flavor.
In a very dark room just one little candle
can bring guidance, hope and cheer.

God calls and qualifies us to be agents of change.
When we are faithful to this calling,
we're a positive influence on lives we touch.
We make the difference God expects of us.

Do It for Jesus

Only once did God walk the earth in the form of man.
As God-man, Jesus did many wonderful things
that demonstrated His divine power.
He stilled the storm, drove out demons, healed the hopeless.

Though He was worthy of being served by angels,
Jesus amazingly was willing to do the job of a servant.

*"Jesus knew that the Father had put all things
under his power . . . so . . ."* (John 13:3-4)
He got up from the meal and washed His disciples' feet.

Jesus did this to set an example,
not only for His disciples, but also for us.
He said, "You also should wash one another's feet."

This does not mean we must be willing to be doormats.
There are times we need to pray for wisdom,
that our loving may be wise,
so the person we serve is really helped.

Wash one another's feet.
Jesus tells us to do a simple thing.

It isn't always easy to put aside our schedule and our pride,
to stoop down and do what needs to be done.

But when we do it "to one of the least of these,"
we do it for Jesus.

How Much Is Enough?

Too often we want to limit our love.
How far are we expected to go?

We ponder the same question a lawyer once
asked Jesus, "Who is my neighbor?"
Does God expect me to help that person?

With Jesus' disciples we ask, "How many times?"
Do I have to forgive this person
who keeps hurting me again and again?

*"Do everything
without complaining or arguing."* (Philippians 2:14)
We must not argue with God —
just do what He tells us to do.

God's Word requires us to love our neighbor.
We need God's guidance to love wisely.
Life is complicated. So is love.

Unqualified Love

Jesus does not say,
"I'll love you if . . ."
"I'll love you when . . ."

Jesus comes
to where you are
and loves you
just as you are.

Don't try to bargain:
"I'll love You if . . ."
"I'll love You when . . ."

Respond, "I love You;
therefore, I'll . . ."

You Have Lovability

What great potential the Lord sees in you!

He sees you as a lovable person
capable of loving others.
He wants to transmit some of His love through you.

You may immediately think of your limitations:
if only I had better health, better education;
more time, more money, more opportunities . . .

Of course, you have some limitations.
But the important thing is that
you capitalize on your potential.

You are God's handiwork.
What He makes is good.
He put you where you are for a purpose.
Make wherever you are a better place.

Don't Put Yourself Down

Job's friend called man *"a worm."* (Job 25:6b)
Some friend! He crushed Job's sagging spirits.

Even King David once felt so low that he wrote,
"I am a worm . . . despised by the people."
(Psalm 22:6)

Most of us have felt pretty low at times.
In a painful moment of rejection we may have groaned:

"I can't do anything right. I'm a failure.
I have nothing worthwhile to offer the world."

When others put us down and step on us,
we may imagine that God, too, sees us as lowly worms.

But the Lord never says we're worms!
His Word tells us He made us a *"little less than God"*
crowned with glory and honor. (Psalm 8:5a RSV)

We must not declare worthless
what God says is of great worth.
We don't bring glory to God by putting ourselves down.

Our daily failure to live up to God's expectations
keeps us humble. We fail, but we're not failures!

We don't have to prove to God we're lovable.
He doesn't demand that we earn His forgiveness.

We do need to repent, to seek His mercy for Jesus's sake.

When we accept God's love and forgiveness, we become new.
As we receive and use His power, we are transformed.

We can make a new start every morning.

Today

We speak of today
as the present.

Today is a present,
a gift from God.

May we live it
gratefully and
wisely.

Some Day Is Here!

Today has never happened before in all eternity.
"This is the day the Lord has made." (Psalm 118:24a)
I will rejoice and be glad in it!

Today is a fragile link between yesterday and tomorrow.
Life is now. This is it!
For all I know this may be all there is.

I cherish happy yesterdays, learn from unhappy ones.
I must not try to relive the past,
but I forget the things which are behind me
and do not worry about what's ahead.

The future is uncertain — even my next step.
I'm not certain of what God will do next.
But I am certain of God.

I belong to a Lord who wants good things for me.
He is here. He is with me. He is in me!

Nothing will happen to me today
that we can't handle together.
I walk by faith knowing God is for me.

I will rejoice and be glad in the Lord today.

Jesus Is Savior and Lord

"What must I do to be saved?" (Acts 16:30b)
The man who asked that was panic stricken.

The answer given him was, *"Believe in the Lord Jesus
and you will be saved . . . "* (Acts 16:31)

Many never ponder that question.
They justify themselves. They work hard,
do the best they can, and don't hurt anybody.
Some are convinced that confirmation and
church membership guarantee passage to heaven.
Others feel they can follow any religious belief
as long as they are sincere.

Jesus says, *"I am the way, and the truth, and the life;
no one comes to the Father, but by me."* (John 14:6 RSV)

What must we do to be saved? Believe in Jesus.
There is nothing else we can do; nothing else we need do.
Jesus did it all. All to Him we owe.

Faith alone! Does this mean we can live as we please?
By no means! *"Faith without deeds is dead."* (James 2:26b)
True faith changes us drastically.

Jesus is our Savior. He is also our Lord and Master.
Because we believe in Him as our Way to heaven,
we follow His way of life here on earth.
We walk as He walked. We do what He commands.

We love and obey Jesus not to be saved.
We love and obey Him because we are saved.

*"Let us
fix
our eyes
on
Jesus."*
  (Hebrews 12:2a)

Sleep in Peace

We sleep one-third of our lives.
That's a large portion of our allotted time!
We know sleep is very important.
That's why it is so frustrating when we can't sleep.

Before going to bed spend time in prayer.
Confess your faults and failures.
Accept God's forgiveness.

Thank the Lord for the day's blessings,
rest assured that your tomorrow
is also in His powerful hand.
"Do not worry about tomorrow" says Jesus. (Matthew 6:34a)
Remind yourself: *"The Lord is my shepherd,
I shall not want."* (Psalm 23:1 RSV)

Think positively. Repeat a thought like:
*"I will lie down and sleep in peace,
for you alone, O Lord, make me dwell in safety."* (Psalm 4:8)

A sleepless hour need not be wasted time.
With the psalmist you can say to the Lord,
*"On my bed I remember you; I think of you
through the watches of the night."* (Psalm 63:6)
Take your mind off yourself, your problems, your plans.
Think about God — how great and good He is.

*"He (Jesus) died for us so that, whether we are awake
or asleep, we may live together with Him."*

(1 Thessalonians 5:10)

Enjoy that togetherness!

I Need to Go to Church

Going to church doesn't make me a Christian
any more than going to a garage makes me a car.

God's children have always gathered to worship Him.
His Word tells us, *"Let us not give up meeting together,
as some are in the habit of doing, but let us encourage
one another . . ."* (Hebrews 10:25)

The church service is a family reunion.
By sharing joys and sorrows we strengthen one another.
We remind each other that our faith in Jesus
makes a difference in our daily struggles.

I need the smiles and hugs of my brothers and sisters in Christ.
They cheer me on my way for the rest of the week.
This is tremendously important for me,
but it is just a fringe benefit.

It takes effort for me to remember:
I go to church primarily to meet my heavenly Father,
to come before His presence with thanksgiving,
and to praise Him in His sanctuary.

It helps me to look at the cross —
not on what is seen, but on what is unseen.
I fix my thoughts on Jesus. He died on a cross
to pay a debt He didn't owe, because I owed a debt I couldn't pay.
He died for me personally. I believe that with all my heart.
Because of what He did, I am God's forgiven child.

Worshiping the Lord with my fellow Christians
renews, restores, rejuvenates me.
It also reminds me that I have been saved to serve.
My heavenly Father is depending upon me
to share His love with those whose lives touch mine.

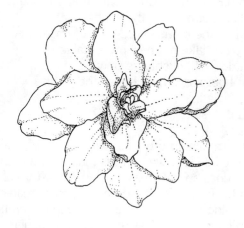

A Confession

When I read the story of the tax collector and the
Pharisee, I identify with the tax collector.
I'm certainly not like the Pharisee.
I never thank God that I'm better than others —
though I must acknowledge I go to church rain or shine,
summer and winter, at home or away.

Yet I must admit that when I arrive in church,
the most important thing on my mind is not my sin.
My mind has been occupied with many thoughts:
Fix breakfast, straighten the kitchen.
Shower, tidy the bathroom. Make the bed.
Dress, try to make my hair presentable.
Drive. Park. Talk, exchange news.
Pray that I get something out of the service.
Read the bulletin.
Sing. Read. Listen.

Suddenly I'm joining others in words of confession,
"Most merciful God, we confess that we are by nature
sinful and unclean. We have sinned against you . . . "
I have to keep up with the others. They're reading fast.
I'm confessing my sinful nature — sin in general.
There isn't time to confess my sins in particular.

"Lord, have mercy." Again and again.
The effect of repetition can be deadening.

I need encouragement. Maybe the sermon
will offer some practical suggestions for my Christian life:
how I can improve my relation to Jesus,
what I could do to share His love with others this week.

It is easier for me to praise the Lord in public worship.
Only in the quiet temple of my heart can I confess my sins.

Jesus, Savior of the world. You have saved me.
Save me now from this sin I'm confessing:
Lord, have mercy on me, a sinner, a modern-day Pharisee.

Busyness Is Not Always God's Business

Dear Jesus,
when You told a parable about people
who failed to show love to a neighbor in need,
You chose to criticize a priest and a Levite —
two people actively involved in religious duties.

Sometimes I'm so busy working hard for You,
that I'm apt to have no patience with
people who distract me from by busyness.

Guide me to make wise choices —
to do what is most important —
not only what is most urgent.

I must not be an activity addict.
Keep me mindful that You are not
looking for a performance from me,
but a relationship with me.

That will affect my relation to
those You place in my path
as I go down my Jericho Road.

You've Been Chosen

In a world where success is calculated
by money, fame, and influence,
you may feel like a nobody —
necessary to no one and noticed by none.

God considers you a somebody!
He says, "... *you are precious in my eyes, and*
honored, and I love you." (Isaiah 43:4a RSV)
You have God's seal of approval!

Did you merit such approval? Not at all.
It is pure grace — undeserved love.
In His amazing mercy God gave His beloved Son
that you might become His child.

God has chosen you. He chooses to use you.
You are accountable to Him
for the special person He has made of you.
What are you doing with His gifts?

No matter what led you to where you are today,
the Lord has a purpose for your life.
Somebody needs to be loved by you.

Jesus says,
*"You did not
choose me,
but I
chose you . . .
to go and
bear fruit —
fruit that
will last. . . . "*
(John 15:16)

Coping with Stress

We are imperfect people sharing an imperfect world
with a lot of other imperfect people.
No wonder we have stress!

Some major stress factors are:
death of a loved one, death of a marriage,
serious sickness or severe injury to self or family,
loss of one's job, moving to a new location,
living or working with people who don't cooperate.

Other stressors are relatively minor by comparison:
an appliance that doesn't work,
rushing to make a deadline or appointment,
doing chores we don't like or have difficulty handling,
waiting in line, driving in heavy traffic.

The Lord equipped our bodies to respond to stress,
providing us with what we need for flight or fight.
When we can do neither, the body suffers.
The result may be headaches, ulcers, even cancer.

We are blessed when we can reach out to family
and friends for support and encouragement.

Exercising the body helps: take a walk, breathe deeply.
Relax. Read. Listen to music.
Do whatever calms us down.

Exercising our faith in God is the best remedy of all.
Faith works when we work it!

Faith allows us to fling ourselves with confidence
into the arms of our loving heavenly Father.
He is our strength. He has helped us to this point.
He will help us handle every situation we may face.

Forgiving Isn't Easy

It is easier to confess our sins
than to admit our faults.

When we offer someone an apology
for an insult or injury,
we often offer it with an explanation.
We admit our action was wrong but
understandable under the circumstances.
We may feel a little guilty,
but may also feel we were justified.

When we stand before God,
it's not enough just to admit we've done wrong.

We can't justify ourselves by reasoning:
I couldn't help it. That's the way You made me.
Everybody else is doing it. Nobody's perfect.

God demands that we repent,
be so sorry for sinning that we want to stop.

God takes our sin seriously.
What an awesome price He paid for our pardon!
He loved us enough to sacrifice His beloved Son!

God in His mercy is willing to forgive us.
We must forgive those who hurt us,
even when they try to justify their actions.

Nothing is more difficult than to forgive.
Nothing is more God-like.

Fear Not

When your knees knock, kneel on them!

Fear helps preserve us.
Only the foolish are fearless.
But fears can also immobilize us,
chaining us in a dungeon of despair.
We dread doing what needs to be done,
refuse to risk what can make life worth living.

God doesn't say, "Fear not. There's nothing to be afraid of."

He does promise:
"Do not fear, for I am with you;
do not be dismayed, for I am your God.
I will strengthen you and help you . . ." (Isaiah 41:10)

God knows what you face and how you feel.
But talking about your fears with Him
helps you be aware of His presence and power.

Thank God for listening.
Affirm your faith in words like these:
Lord, You are my strength. You are in control.
" . . . I will trust and not be afraid. . . . " (Isaiah 12:2)

Thank God for answering.
Believe God's Spirit is in you
giving you the strength and courage you need.

That's faith. Faith gets rid of fear.

Thank God!

Training ourselves to be thankful is good exercise.
It moves us to concentrate on the good things
God has done and is doing for us.

To be thankful for what we have
takes our attention off what we do not have.

The Word of God tells us,
*"Give thanks in all circumstances, for this is
God's will for you in Christ Jesus."* (1 Thessalonians 5:18)

There is no situation in which we
cannot find something to be thankful for.

In the deepest of disappointments or
the most traumatic of tragedies
we are strengthened if we focus on thanking God.

The Lord doesn't expect us to thank Him for bad things,
though once in a while we can see
how something good has come out of evil.

God wants us to thank Him in the midst of circumstances,
even when things make no sense whatsoever to us.
We thank God that He loves us, that He is in control,
and that somehow He will work things out for our good.
This lifts our spirits and gives us hope.

Whenever we worship and whenever we pray,
we need to emphasize thanksgiving.
It helps us remember how great God is,
and how precious we are in His sight!

Weather or Not

We tend to be gloomy when the weather is.
Grumbling about the weather only makes things worse.

To make the best of a poor situation
I never buy a dark umbrella.
On rainy days my bright-colored umbrella cheers me —
and perhaps my little corner of the world.

Too little sunshine affects our attitude.
An attitude is a little thing that makes a big difference.
We can alter our life by altering our attitude.

I can remind myself,
"Jesus wants me for a sunbeam to shine for Him today."
I must let the Son shine through me.

If I think of reasons to give thanks to God,
I'm ready to share them with those
who complain to me about the weather.

Like so many things in life
the weather is beyond my control.
Adjusting can be frustrating, but
I have to learn to live with what God sends.

Happiness Is

I'll be happy when I get . . .
                          get there.
                          get over this.
                          get to be or do . . .

Maybe.
Such happiness doesn't last for long.
There are only happy days or hours.

Life has its ups and downs.
One downer spoils our happiness.

Our loved ones are important to us.
So are things to a lesser extent.

But life does not depend
on our connections or possessions.

Someday each of us will
be separated from everyone we've loved
and everything we've enjoyed in this world.

Then the thing that counts —
the only thing that counts —
is our relation to Jesus.

Be Yourself

Live life in your own skin!
You cannot be what someone else is.
God doesn't expect you to be.

People come in different shapes, sizes, ages.
We differ in looks, likes, intelligence, blessings.
God in His wisdom has given us different kinds of gifts.
Some have many; others, few.

God doesn't compare you with any other person.
He judges what you are by what you ought to be.
He judges what you do by what you could be doing.
He judges you not by the gifts He's given you,
but by your faithfulness in using those gifts.

Accept who you are: a person precious in God's sight.
He wants you to be all you can be.

Thank God for your assets. Work to develop them.
Ask for His help in overcoming your liabilities.

The Lord can do wonderful things
using your unique qualities and experiences.

You're the only person exactly like you.
One thing you can do better than anybody else
and that is: be yourself.

Take Responsibility

What we are today has been greatly influenced
by what has been said and done to us over the years.

Because of the effect people have upon us,
we tend to explain our own failures and faults
by pointing to the imperfections of others.

Parents made mistakes; teachers were not competent;
a doctor or pastor was not wise;
other people were cruel or careless.

These facts may well be true.
They help us understand ourselves —
the way we think, feel, or operate.
But to blame our heredity or our habitat
does not solve problems or improve our life.

The blame game started when Adam blamed Eve.
She said the devil made her do it.
Ultimately they blamed God.

God held them responsible for their actions.
He holds us responsible for our reactions
to whatever life hands us.

Each of us needs to remember:
I am not just a victim of circumstances.
I cannot control everything that happens to me.
I can control only how I respond to it.
This is my life.
I am responsible for it.
I need to do the best I can with what I've got
under the circumstances.

"I call to God,
and the Lord saves me.

Evening, morning and noon
I cry out in distress,
and he hears my voice."
(Psalm 55:16,17)

"God is our refuge
and strength,
an ever-present help
in trouble."
(Psalm 46:1)

You'll Make It

Are things so bad you think you can't go on?
Does the problem before you loom like a big brick wall?

You may feel helpless.
But your situation is never hopeless.

You can take down enough of the wall brick by brick
to climb over, go around, or tunnel through.

Are you secretly blaming God for your trouble?
You can't keep a secret from God.
Talk it over with Him honestly. You'll feel better.
A grudge against God is a very dangerous attitude.
You need His help in facing adversity.

God loves you. He forgives.
He'll give you the strength to make it through today.
Tomorrow He will again enable you.

The Lord often helps through family and friends.
The helping hand or unclouded vision of another person
can help you get started and motivate you to go on.
See God's goodness in the aid given by others.
Your thankful spirit will make it easier for them.

Don't give up. You'll make it.
Little by little you'll experience victory —
satisfaction in removing one brick at a time.

With God's help you can handle anything life offers you.

Expect a Loving Answer

The four-year-old spent the night with his grandparents.
Anxious to please, Grandma asked him,
"What would you like for breakfast?"

He thought and thought, and then replied,
"How about a bowl of M & M's?"

Did he ask in faith? Yes.
Did his grandmother hear him? Yes.
Did she give him what he asked for? No!

Was that proof she didn't love him? Not at all!
It proved she did love him — more than he loved himself.
But she was much wiser than he and saw a broader picture.

Jesus tells us, *"Ask and it will be given to you."* (Matthew 7:7a)
He is not giving us a blank check,
a promise to give us everything our heart desires.
That would put us in control and make Him our Servant.

When we pray, we come before a God who loves us.
We can ask Him for anything.

But sometimes we must be satisfied with the answer "no."

God's ways are higher than our minds.

He Holds Our Hand

It was a busy intersection.
Trucks and busses jostled with cars for position.
But the little two-year-old boy skipped along
laughing excitedly, savoring the commotion.

He didn't have any idea how he'd get across
the street amidst such heavy traffic.
But it didn't worry him.
He was safe and secure clinging to his daddy's hand.
All was well with his world!

Wouldn't it be great if we adults
could face present dangers and the unknown future
with such trust — confident our heavenly Father
is holding our hand!

Word Power

What we are today has been largely shaped by words.
Some of those words we can still recall
often after many, many years.
Others are buried deep in our subconscious mind
exerting a subtle influence on our thinking.

Encouraging words develop self-esteem.
They make us feel secure and significant.
They let us know we are loved and capable of loving.

Too many harsh, critical words crush us.
They so magnify our faults and failures
that we don't see any possibilities in ourselves.

Most of us respond better if we are condemned less
and commended more.

Words of praise lift our spirits,
help us set higher goals and
strive harder to reach them.

Wise words of advice spoken in love
teach us how to cope with life's challenges.

How we influence one another with our words!
We need to choose and use words wisely.

I Am Somebody

Heavenly Father,
at times I wonder,

"Why doesn't somebody do something?"

O Lord, help me realize
I might be that somebody.

When I suffer compassion fatigue,
sharpen my sensitivity to the needs of others.
Make me more conscious of ways
I can reflect Your concern.

Wherever I am,
whatever shape I'm in,
however limited my time or resources,
may I never underestimate
my ability
to make the world
a little better
for someone else.

I cannot do everything.
But I can do something.
With Your help, Lord,
what I can do
I will do.

Living for Jesus

Dear Lord,

You loved me enough
to die for me.

Help me love You enough
to live for You.

What do You want
me to do today?

Open my eyes to recognize
the opportunities You give.

Light of My Life

Jesus is the light of the world.
He says I'm the light of the world, too.

My shining is not to attract attention to me,
but to bring glory to the Lord.

My good works are not to make me look good,
but to be magnets to draw others to Jesus.

"God . . . made his light
shine in our hearts . . .

We have this
treasure
in jars of clay
to show that this
all-surpassing
power is from God
and not from us."
    (2 Corinthians 4:6,7)

" . . . Let your light
shine before men,
that they may see
your good deeds
and praise
your Father in heaven."
(Matthew 5:16)

Go with God

How precious you are to God!

Jesus died for you!
That's a terribly simple statement,
but a simply terrible truth!

God's perfect Son
was sacrificed for your sins!

In this wondrous act of love
the almighty Creator reached down
to draw you to Himself.

He wants to have a growing,
loving, personal relationship with you!

> Therefore,
> be an imitator of God,
> as a dearly loved child
> and live a life of love,
> just as Christ loved you and
> gave Himself up for you
> as a fragrant offering
> and sacrifice to God.
> (from Ephesians 5:1,2)

God
is
for
you!